Marty Gets a Job

by Evan Allen
illustrated by Luciana Navarro Alves

Scott Foresman
is an imprint of

Glenview, Illinois • Boston, Massachusetts • Mesa, Arizona
Shoreview, Minnesota • Upper Saddle River, New Jersey

Illustrations by Luciana Navarro Alves

ISBN 13: 978-0-328-39403-6
ISBN 10: 0-328-39403-3

1 2 3 4 5 6 7 8 9 10 V010 17 16 15 14 13 12 11 10 09 08

Chapter One

Marty Apple was bored. He was usually much too busy with things to be bored. But Marty was not interested in any of the things he usually did. He had cleaned his room, played his video games, and read his books. Somehow it was not enough. His day was too much like the day before. Every day, since summer had started, felt the same. That afternoon Marty made a very important decision.

"I think I need to get a job," Marty told his mom that night.

Marty's mother knew her son needed a change. He needed new friends, new hobbies, and new things to do.

"Well, do you have any ideas in mind, Marty?" Mom asked.

"I don't know, Mom. What do *you* think I would be good at?"

Marty hoped his mother could give him some choices. No matter how hard he tried, he simply couldn't come up with a good idea.

At first he had imagined working as a firefighter. He could spend his days driving his own fire truck all around town, saving grateful townspeople from all sorts of trouble.

"I bet I would never get bored as a fireman!" he said to himself, smiling at the thought of the many great adventures he would have.

But Marty's joy did not last. No matter how exciting the job could be, no one would want to hire an eight-year-old firefighter!

Next Marty thought about being a police officer. He imagined driving through town in a police car, with the lights flashing and the siren blaring. Then he realized no one would hire an eight-year-old police officer either.

Marty could not think of any job an eight-year-old could do, believing he was just too young.

"You've always told me I have a good head on my shoulders. What kinds of jobs are there for someone with a good head?" Marty asked his mom.

"Marty, I think I may have the perfect job for you," Mrs. Apple said thoughtfully. Just yesterday, her boss had told her he needed volunteers to help at the hospital.

To Mrs. Apple's surprise, Marty frowned when she suggested working at the hospital. "I already thought of that! I'm too young to be a firefighter, a police officer, or a doctor!"

Mrs. Apple laughed. "That's true that being a doctor would not be possible right now. I was thinking you could work as a volunteer in the children's ward. It's a lot of responsibility, but I believe you can handle it."

Mrs. Apple explained that Marty would be helping by spending some time with the youngest patients. He could read to them, play board games with them, or just chat and keep them company.

"So . . . I'd be helping the kids in the hospital get better?" Marty got more excited as he thought about the idea. "That sounds *almost* like being a doctor! Can I start tomorrow, Mom?"

"I know it's exciting, Marty. Your first job is a big deal, but you know you still have to do your chores at home, right?"

Marty had forgotten all about his chores. Every day, he had to clean his room and do the dishes. Marty knew these jobs were very important to his mom, and he promised her he wouldn't forget them.

Chapter Two

The next day, Mrs. Apple brought Marty to meet her boss, Mr. Garcia.

"Congratulations, Marty, you're our newest assistant!" Mr. Garcia welcomed him. "On Monday morning you'll start your first day of volunteering."

"Thanks! I'll be the best volunteer you've ever had," Marty grinned.

Marty was so excited on Monday that he woke up even before his mom. Leaving his pajamas on the floor of his room, he changed into his clothes and went down to breakfast.

Mrs. Apple came into the kitchen as Marty was finishing his cereal. She watched Marty as he bounced in his seat, his eyes wide with excitement.

"I am so proud of you!" Mrs. Apple reached out to hug her son.

"Stop, Mom! You're going to wrinkle my shirt!" Marty said, squirming.

Marty's first day as a volunteer passed by like a whirlwind. Marty met Nurse Tiant, who showed him around. At first Marty felt a little nervous, but Nurse Tiant was very friendly, and he made Marty laugh. Soon, Marty felt much more comfortable.

Marty followed Nurse Tiant everywhere as he made his rounds and introduced Marty to all the boys and girls in the children's ward.

For the rest of the day, Marty spent a little time with every child. He made a lot of new friends. Before Marty knew it, his mom was there to take him home. He spent the entire bus ride talking about his wonderful day.

By the time they got home, Marty was very tired. He stumbled past the pair of pajamas on his bedroom floor and tumbled into bed, exhausted.

Chapter Three

Marty enjoyed volunteering at the hospital more and more each day. Everyone liked Marty, and Nurse Tiant told Mrs. Apple that Marty was one of the best volunteers the hospital had ever had.

Mrs. Apple was pleased by the kind words, but she was noticing some troubling things at home. She was starting to worry.

Marty seemed to be giving more and more of his attention to his volunteer work. Mrs. Apple could not remember the last time she had seen Marty clean his room. Marty was doing the one thing he had promised not to do. He was neglecting his chores.

Marty had stopped doing the dinner dishes, and his dirty clothes were piling up. Mrs. Apple was worried that soon they would both forget what the floor of Marty's bedroom looked like!

That Friday, Mrs. Apple decided that she and Marty would take off early from the hospital and go on a picnic.

"Marty," Mrs. Apple said, when they were at the park, "You know that everyone at the hospital loves having you there, right? I've gotten nothing but good reports about you."

"Yeah, Mom, its been great! Nurse Tiant is really cool," Marty said. "And I've made so many new friends!"

"That's good, Marty, but we need to talk about how this is working out."

"I am very proud of you," Mrs. Apple continued. "But at the same time, you and I both know you haven't been keeping up with your chores at home."

"I'm sorry," Marty said, looking at the ground.

"It's OK. I accept your apology. But maybe you are spending a little too much time volunteering."

"But, Mom, I love it!" Marty cried.

"I know, but I think we have to make a few changes," Mrs. Apple said quietly.

Mrs. Apple told Marty he would need to spend fewer hours at the hospital. She explained that she wanted him to have more time at home. That way, he could do his chores, play his games, read his books, and enjoy all the things he had enjoyed doing before.

"That doesn't sound so bad, does it?" Mrs. Apple asked.

Marty thought about how much he had missed his old friends. It might be good to have time to do the things he used to do.

"No, I guess not," he replied, starting to trust his mom's judgment. "But I can still keep my job, right?"

"Yes, of course you can still keep your job," Mrs. Apple smiled.

"OK," Marty said, giving his mom a hug. "Mom, you're the best!"

"And *you're* the best!" replied Mrs. Apple, ruffling Marty's hair. "You're the best son and the best volunteer!"

Making A Responsible Choice

In this story, Marty was so busy that he stopped doing his chores. It was important to Marty's mom that he did his chores because she wanted Marty to learn to be responsible.

Do you have any chores to do at home? Why is being responsible important? How can being responsible help other people?